The Law of Prayer:

Understanding the Kingdom Protocol of Petition

Part of the Kingdom Teaching Mini-book Series

Dr. J.C. Matthews

J.C. Matthews International Publishing

P.O. Box 1083
Keller, Texas 76244
www.jcmatthews.international

Printed in the United States of America
All Scripture quotations are taken from The King James Version
(KJV) of the Holy Bible, unless otherwise noted.

Scripture quotation marked 'NKJV" are taken from the New King
James Version® . Copyright © 19 8 2 by Thomas Nelson, Inc. .
Used by per mission. All rights reserved .

Scripture quotations marked (NIV) are taken from the HOLY
BIBLE, NEW INTERNATIONAL VERSION®. NIV ®. Copyright ©
1973, 1978, 1984 by International Bible Society. Used by
permission of Zondervan. All rights reserved.

"Scripture quotations marked (AMP) are taken from the
Amplified® Bible, Copyright © 1954, 1958, 1962, 1964, 1965, 1987
by The Lockman Foundation . Used by permission."
(www.Lockman.org)

*The Law of Prayer: Understanding the Kingdom's Protocol of
Petition*

ISBN 13: 978-0-9792554-3-4 ISBN 10: 0-9792554-3-0
Copyright© 2015 Dr. J.C. Matthews

J.C. Matthews International
P.O. Box 1083
Keller, Texas 76244
www.jcmatthews.international

Published by J.C. Matthews International
Visit or site at: www.jcmatthews.international

Table of Contents

Introduction

Most Christians agree that prayer is an important component of believer's life. However, if we were honest, most of us would admit that we are not confident in our prayers being answered. This lack of confidence is the consequence of their past experience in their prayers having been ineffective and having gone unanswered. As a result, many have become frustrated and come to the conclusion that prayer simply doesn't work. This should not be our testimony, about something the Bible says that we ought to do without ceasing.

Prayer is one of the most important activities we as believers can participate. It is a privilege granted by God, that if understood, could not only transform our lives, but the world we live in. Prayer, when properly understood is one of the most rewarding and powerful experiences a believer can have. I believe a majority of the frustration believers encounter when praying is a consequence of our: (1) possessing an improper perspective of what prayer truly is, (2) never having received any real instruction on the different kinds of prayer, (3) lacking understanding of the purpose of prayer, and (4) our approaching prayer exclusively as a religious activity, and not understanding its true purpose.

The Bible teaches that effective prayer is something that must be learned. This is why the Bible says that Jesus had to teach His disciples to pray (Luke 11:1). Prayer is not, as it is popularly taught, simply holding a conversation with God. If this were the case, there would be no need to be taught how to pray, we would just talk to God. It is important to note that before Jesus began to teach His disciples on the proper way to pray, He drew their attention to what was currently accepted as prayer, and warned them not to pray in that manner. Specifically, He warned them:

> *"But when ye pray, use not vain repetitions, as the heathen do: for they think that they shall be heard for their much speaking. Be not ye therefore like unto them: for your Father knoweth what things ye have need of, before ye ask him" (Matthew 6:7-8).*

He then begins to give them a blueprint for effective prayer. This blueprint directs the disciples focus on the true purpose of prayer, while revealing several laws and principles that govern this very important privilege we've been given. Jesus' model prayer taught a specific order and priority, which is the key to having effective prayer. Jesus' prayer paved the way for man to regain access to heaven and heaven to earth.

To properly utilize the privilege of prayer, we must gain an understanding of:

1. What truly is prayer?
2. What is the origin of prayer?
3. Why is it necessary that we pray?
4. How do my prayers impact God's ability to intervene in my life?

Prayer is both a right and responsibility possessed by every citizen of God's Kingdom. It is a privileged communication that must contain the proper reverence, respect and foundation for us to have confidence in our prayers being answered.

It must be noted that there are several kinds of prayers mentioned in the Bible. There are prayers of intercession, supplication, repentance, thanksgiving and so on. For the purpose of this book, I will be focusing on one of the most popular kinds of prayer found in the Bible and used in the Body of Christ today. This is the *"prayer of petition"*. The *prayer of petition* is one in which the individual seeks God's intervention, to do something on their behalf. The model prayer Jesus taught His disciples, also called the "Lord's Prayer", falls into this category of prayer. From this perspective, we will discover how the Bible and Jesus Himself said that we should pray. This revelation will revolutionize, not only how we pray but what we pray for!

As a final note, as we turn to engage our study on prayer as a petition, I wanted to share with you why I am writing this book and why it is so important to me. I am writing this book and others like it, from the perspective of being first a Christian, pastor, leader, as well as, a student and graduate of law school. My area of concentration was *Labor and Employment law*, with an emphasis on contracts. This area of law requires great detail to the meaning of words and an understanding of relationships between parties involved in an agreement. As I began to read the Bible I found myself coming across numerous legal terms, concepts, principles and even laws that I studied as a student in law school. Some of the more difficult to understand text in the Bible became very clear when I viewed them from a legal perspective, and not a religious one. Scriptures such as Isaiah 43:26, where God says to bring Him in remembrance of His word and to state our case. Why would God need us to bring Him, who knows all things, into remembrance of what He has previously said? Surely, God does not have lapses in memory. Why is He commanding the prophet to present a case before Him? As I reflected upon this, I remembered, that this is exactly what a judge does in their courtroom. Judges are generally the most knowledgeable person in the courtroom of the law, but require, as protocol, that those coming before the court cite and present the law in support of their case. Similarly, in 1John 5:14-15, we are told:

> *"Now this is the confidence that we have in Him, that if we ask anything according to His will, He hears us. And if we know that He*

hears us, whatever we ask, we know that we
have the petitions that we have asked of Him."

Again, the imagery is that of a plaintiff bringing their cause before a judge. They have confidence in their petition being granted because it is grounded in what the court has already declared as being so. This would indicate that effective prayer, especially those requesting that something be done for the one praying, requires knowledge of a protocol, our set of principles, by which prayers of petition are made.

I've witnessed the impact of unanswered prayer upon believers who prayed fervently and sincerely over a matter. Many of these believers have fallen away from the faith or become embittered due to their prayers not being answered. They've concluded that either God does not exist or that He doesn't care about them or the things that pertains to their lives. I recognized a need for a study of prayer that focused on the concepts, laws and principles established by God to give us confidence in our prayers being answered. God established these laws to maintain and manifest His will in the earth and to govern His interaction with man. There are things that God cannot do for us because He has legally delegated as man's responsibility.

There are other prayers that we pray that God cannot answer because He has already provided the answer to the prayer, but it requires our having discernment to recognized that which has been provided to address the present need.

Everything we do in this physical world involves the interaction of various laws that determine our success or failure in our natural and spiritual pursuits. These laws work in coordination with one another to ensure consistent outcomes for those who engage them, and to fulfill the predetermined purposes of our Creator for all things. They are given to us so that we can have confidence in the things of God, and to assist us in experiencing the fullness of life God has planned for us. It is only when we recognize that there is an order within God's Kingdom, that if we seek it first, then all things become available and are even added to us, will we begin to experience the life more abundantly that belongs to us.

Chapter One

What is Prayer?

Many believe that prayer is simply our holding a conversation with God. This is at one level true, but I believe that this is an over simplification, if not a limitation upon our understanding of what prayer truly is. In a general sense, prayer can be defined as a means of communication with God, but it is also a *special form* of communication, between heaven and earth that serves a much greater purpose in the plan of God than simply talking with Him.

As believers, viewing prayer as a means of communicating or talking to God is an elementary perspective, due to the fact that God knows our hearts and minds; therefore, there is nothing that we could reveal to Him that He is not already aware of. Jesus makes this clear, when He told His disciples that the:

> *"Father knows the things you have need of before you ask Him. In this manner, therefore, pray ..." (Matthew 6:8, NKJV).*

We will discover that speaking with God is an aspect of prayer that we have been given the privilege of participating in, but it is not the sum of its purpose. Prayer is a provision given man that equips him to partner with God in the realization of God's original and ultimate purpose for the earth and mankind. The purpose is the manifestation of His heavenly Kingdom in the earth in partnership with His sons! You will hear me repeat this often throughout this book, and in others, because having an understanding of this purpose helps us place the rest of scripture in its proper context. Knowing this purpose will give us a higher level of appreciation of who we are in the plan of God as well as, giving us greater understanding of certain events we witness in scripture.

Let Them Have Dominion

I believe the reason the disciples were so unsure of how to pray, was due to the difference they observed in the way Jesus prayed and how those in the religious community prayed. Jesus understood that there were certain principles and laws that governed how God could relate to man and man with God. In order for God to do something "for man" or "in his stead", He has to observe certain self-imposed laws that regulate what He can or cannot do. Jesus understood the impact of God's grant of dominion to mankind, in Genesis 1:26-28, and man's subsequent loss of the Kingdom due to Adam's sin. Dominion can be defined as "absolute authority or sovereignty over a domain or territory". By giving man "absolute or sovereign" authority over the earth, God literally made man the "king" or "ruler" over the earth. Therefore, God's delegation of sovereign authority over the earth, meant that He would have to partner with man, from that point forward to manifest His will in the earth. With this self-imposed limitation placed on what God can do in the earth without the direct participation of a human being in mind, Jesus' approached prayer from a different perspective than those who viewed prayer as being strictly a religious activity. He saw it as a partnership in realizing God's will in the earth. Therefore, He emphasized this when He taught them to pray first:

> "Your kingdom come. Your will be done on earth as it is in heaven" (Matthew 6:10, NKJV).

Man's grant of dominion, was to facilitate his purpose of advancing God's Kingdom in the earth. However, when man spiritually died, he could no longer partner with God or participate in this purpose, with him having lost his citizenship in God's Kingdom. When man spiritually died he not only lost his place in God's Kingdom, but also his ability to connection and spiritually communicate with God was also lost.

The Consequence of the Fall

Let me explain. Prior to the fall of man in the Garden, God spoke openly with him. Man was God's spiritual

son created in His image and likeness. They
communed Spirit to spirit. Adam knew the mind of
God because the Holy Spirit revealed all things to his
spirit, even the deep things of God.

The Apostle Paul recognized this reality in the life
of the born again believer, when he wrote:

> *"Eye has not seen, nor ear heard, nor have
> entered into the heart of man the things which
> God has prepared for those who love Him.' But
> God has revealed them to us through His Spirit.
> For the Spirit searches all things, yes, the deep
> things of God. ¹¹ For what man knows the
> things of a man except the spirit of the man
> which is in him? Even so no one knows the
> things of God except the Spirit of God. ¹² Now
> we have received, not the spirit of the world, but
> the Spirit who is from God, that we might know
> the things that have been freely given to us by
> God." (1Corinthians 2:9-12, NKJV).*

When man disobeyed God and obeyed Satan, he in
effect, declared his *independence* from God and God's
government. This *"declaration of independence"*
required that God separate Himself and His Kingdom
from man, leaving man to care for himself. This left
man to fend for himself against the curse upon the
ground, nature and fallen spiritual realities, which

now where vying for rule of the earth. Man, for the first time, being *"self-sufficient"* quickly discovered that he was *"insufficient"* without God. This revelation is recorded in Genesis 3:10, where man having lost the benefits of citizenship in the Kingdom, for the first time declared that he, *"was afraid" and "naked"*. Fear, lack and insufficiency were now a concern for man in his newfound independence. With God's presence having been removed from man, and man having to struggle to have his needs met, it was now necessary for man to find a way to again gain access to his Source - God.

It is at this point, that we begin to understand the reason prayer, as we know it today, developed. Prayer became the means by which men petitioned God for their needs to be met. It is a response to man's separation and loss of access to God and His government – the Kingdom!

The Principle of Authority

The *Principle of Authority* can be articulated as:

Those who submit themselves to authority become beneficiaries of that authority.

In other words, our submission to authority causes the influence of that authority to become active in our lives. This is why most countries require, as a condition of citizenship, that its citizens take some form of a *pledge of allegiance* to it. They agree to submit to and recognize the laws and sovereignty of their nation.

This submission to the nation's authority entitles the citizen to certain benefits of that nation. The necessity of submission to authority will become more evident as we examine further the role of God's grant of dominion to man plays in our prayers being answered. However, it is important to understand the fact that the Kingdom, at its foundation is a government that operates by law and according to "authority".

Submission to Authority = Benefits

Those who approached the Kingdom with an understanding of authority had their expectations met, regardless of their religious affiliation or belief because they understood authority. In the Gospels we find several people that approached Jesus for non-religious reasons and received what they were in need of, not because they confessed Him as their personal savior, but appealed to His Lordship or His authority over a matter.

An example can be found in the gospel of Matthew, were we find a Roman Centurion who had a very ill servant and approached Jesus to heal his servant (See Matthew 8:5-13). The first thing we must notice is that he did not approach Jesus as a religious figure, by calling Him *Rabbi* as the Pharisee Nicodemus did, when he came to Jesus by night (John 3:2). No. The centurion approached Jesus and addressed Him as *"Lord"*. This is significant, because it was unlawful for him to refer to anyone, especially a non-Roman superior, in this manner. In addressing Jesus as Lord, the Centurion acknowledged and submitted himself to Jesus as one having final authority over the matter. When Jesus agreed to come to the man's house to heal the servant, he replied that it was not necessary because he understood how *authority* worked being someone under authority. The Bible says Jesus marveled at this and said the centurion had *"great faith"*, and that this kind of faith He had not witnessed in all of Israel. The centurion's servant was healed instantly!

Another examples of the Principle of Authority at work is found in another text where someone appeals to Jesus' authority, and not for their own salvation. Like the centurion, the miracle that this individual desired was not for themselves, but someone they had authority over. Specifically, in Matthew 15:21-28, there was a Canaanite woman who had a daughter who was demon possessed. Mark reveals that this woman was a Syrian, who were infamous for idol worship. This woman approached Jesus not for salvation, but on the bases of Him having authority over demons. Upon meeting Jesus she appeals to Him as One having authority by calling Him "Lord" and "Son of David". She indicates her submission to His authority prostrating herself before Him, as one would do a king. Jesus, initially dismisses and disqualifies the woman on religious grounds, but subsequently relents to her persistence, and points to her faith in His authority, as the reason for her daughter's deliverance. As a matter of fact, He declared that she had "great faith"! Again, she received what she requested, not as a consequence of her religious conviction, but her understanding of the Principle of Authority: *The authority you submit to, you have a right to the benefits that flows from that authority.*

Finally, in Matthew 9:27-29 and 20:29-34, we find two sets of blind men seeking Jesus for healing. In both instances the blind men address Jesus as *"Lord"* and *"Son of David"* or *"King"*. None of these are religious titles. In each case, these men recognized Jesus as One who possessed authority over their situation, and as they submitted to that authority they received the benefits of being under it as well!

It is interesting to note, there are only 2 instances in the gospels where Jesus referred to someone's faith as being "great", and in both cases they were non-Jews and not part of the religious community. These two were the Roman Centurion and the Syro-Phoenician woman! In my upcoming book entitled "The Law of Faith" we discuss this revelation in more detail.

The Government of God

It is not a coincidence that God chose and established a kingdom form of government for man to live under in the earth, and not a democracy, republic or any other form of government. One of the things that God did not give man dominion over was other people. These other forms of government set men over other men, instead of all men being subject to the same God. However, when man sinned and lost God's Kingdom, government by and of men became necessary to check man's fallen nature. But this was not God's original intention. It is important to remember that God chose a kingdom for man to live in because it speaks of how we are expected to approach Him. God is not a CEO, Dictator, President, Pope or Priest – He is a King, who happens to also be Our Father! Therefore, we must keep this in mind when we approach Him.

Reciprocal Duties

Having established that we have been placed within a government called the Kingdom of God, we recognize that we are also citizens. Every citizen of a kingdom has three primary or "reciprocal duties" that are part of their covenant with the nation or sovereign to which they belong. These duties are owed in exchange for the corresponding benefits provided by the nation or sovereign to their citizens. These duties are:

1. Allegiance
2. Obey and uphold the sovereign's laws
3. Support the advancement of the kingdom.

These duties apply to every citizen of a kingdom. Likewise, the sovereign owes their citizen the reciprocal duties of:

1. Provision
2. Protection
3. Identity and purpose

As long as the other party upholds their duty toward

the other, they have a right to receive the corresponding benefits of the relationship. Prior to Adam's sin, when he surrendered his allegiance to God by obeying Satan, violating God's law concerning the tree of the knowledge of good and evil and forfeited his place and purpose as ruler of the earth, all of his needs were met (provision), he had not need of protection, and was recognized as the king of the earth. However, when he failed at upholding his duty towards God, he realized that he had lost the benefits of God's provision, protection and purpose. Immediately after the fall, we witness Adam make the following statements, which indicates that he no longer had access to his benefits:

> *"I heard thy voice in the garden, and I was afraid, because I was naked; and I hid myself"*
> *(Genesis 3:10).*

Adam, recognized that he lost his benefits when He said:

- *"I was afraid"* – in need of *protection*
- *"I was naked"* – in need of *provision*, and
- *"I hid myself"* –loss of his identity and purpose by his hiding from His Father.

As a result of Adam's fall he was now responsible for working for the things he needed instead of simply receiving them as part of His Covenant with God and His Kingdom. This is what Jesus referred to when He instructed His disciples not to worry about what they would, eat, drink, wear or even there lives, but to seek first God's Kingdom and His righteousness and all those things would be added to them (Matthew 6:33). As citizens of God's Kingdom it is part of their benefits.

Chapter Two

Prayer As A Petition

"Now this is the confidence that we have in Him,
that if we ask anything according to His will,
He hears us. And if we know that He hears us,
whatever we ask, we know that we have the
petitions that we have asked of Him."
1John 5:14-15 (NKJV)

Prayer is not a reward - it's a right! Citizens have a right to petition their government or nation to redress a wrong or to receive benefits due them by virtue of their citizenship. Often, a citizen's benefits have indeed been provided them by their government, but they have been unjustly withheld or denied due to intermediaries or adversaries encountered along the way. In these cases, the citizen must notify the government of the interruption in their receipt of what belongs to them, and the government becomes responsible for making sure the interruption is removed. Therefore, prayer in this sense would not be for the purpose of getting the government to do something, but for it to exert it's power in making sure what it has promised and provided manifests in the life of those they were intended for. From a kingdom perspective, this is our perception of prayer. We understand that God has already provided for all of our needs. Our prayer is not to protest that God has not provided, but for our government to employ its power to make sure that its promises and provision are realized in our lives.

Because many people view prayer as a religious activity, they also view God's answer to prayer as being a reward for their behavior or zeal in prayer. If they emotionally feel as if they do not deserve something, then they won't pray. However, the truth is, their benefits or right to a thing, has nothing to do with how they feel. Our right is not based upon our worthiness, but rather upon our citizenship! When we approach prayer from a rewards mentality, instead of from a rights mindset, we can never have confidence in the outcome of our prayers.

Petitions

To begin, any prayer in which a request is being made of God to do something for us, or on our behalf, is a *prayer of petition*. The word *petition* is a legal term that describes a formal request addressed to a court, judge or authorized body that contains procedural elements that concluded with a specific request for relief. This request for *relief* is what is known as the *"prayer"*. The prayer is the portion of a petition that specifically sets out what it is the petitioner is expecting the court or one in authority to do for them, based on the rights granted them in law.

This form of pleading, within a kingdom context, was necessary because no one within the kingdom had the power to compel the king to do anything. Therefore, the citizens could not demand anything of the king, but could simply "pray" that he be pleased to see his will done within his kingdom. Therefore, the prayer of petition is really a respectful way of demanding relief of the king, while not dishonoring him.

The Word of a King

In a kingdom, the king's word is law. If a king spoke words concerning a matter, it was the law for the matter. The king, if a righteous one, would not break his word, for it represented the king himself. Therefore, when a petitioner or citizen, brings a matter before a king, they are in effect bringing before the king, his own words.

As a matter of protocol, in order to be heard by the king, the citizen had to: (1) be invited, (2) establish that their request is founded upon an existing law declared by the king, (3) relate the requested remedy to the well being of the king, the kingdom or his integrity, and (4) then conclude by praying that the *king's will be done* concerning the matter.

Why is this important? It is important because our religious notion of prayer is primarily focused on having "our will" done, instead of God's will being done. God is not obligated to answer these kinds of prayers. That's right - God is not obligated to answer prayers that are not founded in His word and purposes.

What I am about to say may come as a surprise to some, but it is a truth that sheds light on the reason so many of our prayers go unanswered: God is does not answer our prayers because we have a need, but to honor and uphold His word. The reason for this is, God has already provided for every need we could possibly have. In order to meet one of our needs, God would not need to create it for us, because it can be found here on earth in someone else's possession. Therefore, our issue is not truly one of God needing to provide us with something, but our seeking the wisdom to come into possession of that which God has already provided. This will become more evident as we examine the concepts, laws and principles surrounding our prayer's as citizens of God's Kingdom.

A petition can be summarized as containing:

1. **Jurisdictional Statement**, which recognizes the court's authority to hear the matter

2. **Statement Personal Jurisdiction or Standing**. The petitioner establishes their right to bring their causes before the court.

3. **Recitation of the Law**. This focuses the courts attention on the legal basis of the petition's claim, to which the petitioner claims to have the right to ask the court to act on their behalf.

4. **Application of Facts.** The petitioner demonstrates how their situation falls within the protections given by the law.

5. **Prayer:** The petitioner, having establishes all of the above, makes a formal demand for relief by the court acting on their behalf in order to uphold the law it established.

I hope I've kindled your curiosity to read further. I am praying that the revelation received in our study of "The Law of Prayer" will revolutionize your prayer lives and cause God's will to be done on earth as it already is in heaven!

Chapter Three

The *Law* in Prayer

"God's Word is Law"

In Matthew chapter 6, when Jesus gave His disciples instructions on how to pray, the prayer He taught them contained several laws and principles that govern man's approach to God and ultimately God's response to man. Many of these principles and laws were established from the very beginning when God created man and placed him within a kingdom, in which man was to live and rule. Other laws and principles were subsequently implemented as a consequence of man's spiritual death and need for God's help concerning his protection, provision and purpose in life.

When man fell, he spiritually died, and was no

longer able to communicate with God, as he was created to do. Therefore, he began to develop a system of rituals surrounding his prayers to God to try and regain what he lost. This is where religious practices were developed in man's attempt to reconnect with God. The word "religion" testifies to this in its etymology. The prefix *"re"* means to *"do again or return to a former state"*, while the second word comprising religion is *"ligion"*, means *"to tie or bind"*. It shares the same root as the word *"ligature"*, which carry the meaning *to tie or bind together*. Therefore, *"re-ligion"* is man's attempt to *"rebind"* or himself to God and restore the relationship and benefits he lost when he sinned and lost the Kingdom.

Rights vs. Rewards

As a result of this separation, man began to try to appease God through various works and rituals in an effort to receive something from God. This form of prayer and worship was found in many of the pagan nations that God's people came into contact with and was subsequently incorporated into their understanding of prayer and worship. These pagan nations believed they had to do something in order to appease their god.. The more extreme the act, the more they appeased their god. As a result, God's people began to approach prayer from a religious perspective, viewing God's response to them as a "reward" for something they did or did not do, instead of it being a "right" that is born out of their relationship with God.

Rights flow from being in right standing with God. This can only be achieved through being in covenant with God. Rights are a product of our being in covenant with God, while rewards are a form of compensation for work done. Sons have rights, while strangers seek rewards.

Understanding Dominion

"Without God man cannot, and without man God will not."

Jesus tells His disciples in Matthew 6:8 that they do not need to engage in long or repetitious prayer concerning their needs because, *"Your Father knows the things you have need of before you ask Him"*. Jesus repeats this at Matthew 6:32, when He charges His disciples not to worry about what they will eat, drink, or wear because God already knows what they have need of. With this in mind, the question must be asked: *"If God already knows what we have need of, why doesn't He simply meet them for us?* This question has vexed believers and unbelievers for centuries. Some believers have even fallen away from the faith, concluding that prayer does not work or that, God either does not exist or does not care about our temporal lives. Of course this is not true. However, to answer these concerns and questions, we must first understand the laws and principles established by God to govern the relationship between Himself and man.

"Let Them"

When God, in Genesis 1:26 and 28, said *"Let them have dominion ... over all the earth"*, He effectively limited what He could do in the earth without the participation of a human being. God did not say *"Let*

Us" have dominion, but excluded Himself when He said *"Let them"*.

When God spoke these words, He for all intents and purposes, legally turned control of the earth and its affairs over to human beings. This grant of dominion became the law by which God interacts with man on the earth. There can only be one sovereign ruling over a territory. God, being the Sovereign *owner* of the earth, granted man complete authority over it, as a steward who will be held accountable for his stewardship of what has been given him. Even in this grant of dominion to man, God always intended that He would lead man in his decision making process through His indwelling Spirit. However, when man spiritually died, this was not possible, and man was lift to his own fallen intellect and will for direction.

Self -Imposed Limitations

This declaration of "dominion" literally made it illegal for God to interfere in the affairs of man without the participation of a human being. The writer of the book

of Hebrews commented on this grant of dominion when
he wrote:

> *"What is man that You are mindful of him,*
> *Or the son of man that You take care of him?'*
> *… 'You have put all things in subjection*
> *under his feet." For in that He put all in*
> *subjection under him, He left nothing that is*
> *not put under him"* (Hebrews 2:6-8, NKJV).

This writer of Hebrews, was actually quoting Psalms
chapter 8, which reads:

> *"What is man that You are mindful of him,*
> *And the son of man that You visit him?" … 'You*
> *have made him to have dominion over the*
> *works of Your hands; You have put all things*
> *under his feet"* (Ps. 8:4-6, NKJV).

The text declares that God left *nothing*, as it pertains
to the earth, outside of man's dominion and control.
Having established man as the sovereign in the earth,
God must await the submission of a human beings will,
through which to manifest His will in the earth.

"God Needs Some--Body"

Whenever we see God desiring to do something in the

earth, He always seeks a man to do it through. An excellent illustration of God acknowledging the Law of Dominion is found in the book of Exodus where He desires to deliver His people from Egyptian bondage. Specifically the text reads:

"And the Lord said: "I have surely seen the oppression of My people who are in Egypt, and have heard their cry because of their taskmasters, for I know their sorrows. So I have come down to deliver them out of the hand of the Egyptians, and to bring them up from that land to a good and large land, to a land flowing with milk and honey' .... "Come now, therefore, and I will send you to Pharaoh that you may bring My people, the children of Israel, out of Egypt" (Exodus 3:7-10, NKJV).

It is evident that God desires to deliver His people, and even states that He has come down to do exactly that. However, He turns to Moses and says that He is sending him to Pharaoh to bring His people out. God basically said to Moses: *"**I've** heard the cries of My people. **I've** come down to deliver them from bondage; however, I'm not a man, neither do I have a body. Therefore Moses, I need **you** to go for me because I have men dominion over the earth realm. I am Spirit and* *must find a man who will yield his will to Mine, so that I can manifest My will in the earth."*

We witness God' recognizing the need for Him to be a man with a physical body in order to impact the affairs of men in the earth, when He sent His Son Jesus to save mankind. In the book of Hebrew, the writer records, the Son words, when He said:

"Therefore, when He came into the world, He said: "Sacrifice and offering You did not desire, But a body You have prepared for Me" (Hebrews 10:5).

God prepared the Son a body, to be born as a man so that He could legally represent man and fulfill the will of God in the earth, just as God intended for the first Adam to do.

God's Body

God, from the beginning, intended that He would have access to the earth through the medium of a Spirit filled man or woman. This is why we are created with a place reserved for God within us. We were meant to house the presence of God. The Apostle Paul confirms this when writing to the church at Corinth. Specifically, he said:

> *"Foods for the stomach and the stomach for foods' ... 'Now the body is not for sexual immorality but for the Lord, and the Lord for the body" (1 Corinthians 6:13).*

Paul said, just as the stomach is created to receive food, our bodies were created to receive and house the Spirit of God. Once we are born again, God takes residence within us so that He can legally carryout His will in the earth. Again, Paul makes this point when he wrote:

> *"Know ye not that ye are the temple of God, and that the Spirit of God dwelleth in you?" (1Corinthians 3:16).*

It must be noted that God still must respect the will of man, even though He lives within us. He will not hijack our will in order to manifest His. He will simply seek someone else, who will submit their will to His, through which He can legally manifest His in the earth. We are the body, the body of Christ, God uses to manifest His will in the earth!

It is important to remember this principle when

we are looking for answers as to why our prayer are, or are not, answered. When God answers our prayers, our answer will not simply fall out of the sky, but must be manifested through another human being's actions and obedience. God uses human beings to manifest the answer to our prayers.

Remember this principle: *In order for manifestation to occur, it must involve a man.* You cannot say the word *"manifestation"* without *first* saying the word *"man"!*

Understanding Ownership

Contrary to popular believe, when God granted man dominion over the earth, He did not covey to him *ownership*, but stewardship. They may appear the same, looking from the outside in, but they are very different. Owners have the right of disposition of their possession, and are not accountable to a higher authority for it. Stewards have the right of possession, on behalf of the owner, and can exercise ownership like authority over the property, to all but the owner. The steward is accountable to the owner, and cannot dispose of the owner's property as they see fit. He is a representative of the owner to the world, concerning the possession.

The Bible declares that, *"the earth is the Lord's, and the fullness thereof, the world, and they that dwell therein"* (Psalms 24:1). God is the owner of it all! He is the Landlord and we are tenants who have been granted the right to enjoy possession of what God owns.

Landlord & Tenant

When God conveyed the right of dominion to man, He transferred to man the right to occupy, possess, and enjoy the uses of His property, with the right to rule it on His behalf. However, God retained to Himself the title to the earth.

To truly understand the relationship between God, man and His will being done on earth, in light of His grant of dominion to man, I will be using the relationship between a *landlord and tenant* to illustrate how God and man interact with one another in exercising authority over the earth.

I know, by now you're thinking to yourself: *"What does all of this have to do with prayer?"* My answer is: *"Everything!"* These laws and principles give us insight on understanding how and on what basis does God respond to our prayers concerning things that relate to the affairs of men on the earth.

Covenant

To begin, God chose the vehicle of covenant to relate to mankind. I believe He did so because covenants do not necessarily require the consent, or even the knowledge, of those who will be beneficiaries of the covenant.

A second characteristic of a true covenant is that it is irrevocable. Once a covenant is confirmed by an oath, it is enforceable until fulfilled. The reason man retained authority over the earth after his fall was due to the Adamic Covenant God established with man. The word Adam is a formal identification of the human race. The word "adam", means "man". This is evidenced in Genesis 5 where Moses records:

> *"This is the book of the generations of Adam.*
> *In the day that God created man, in the*
> *likeness of God made he him;2 Male and*
> *female created he them; and blessed them, and*
> *called their name Adam, in the day when they*
> *were created."*

The NIV translation of the Bible renders the word "man" as "mankind". This of course is in reference to Genesis 1:27, where:

> *"God created man in his own image, in the*
> *image of God created he him; male and female*
> *created he them."*

In both cases the word "man" is a direct reference, not the *male-man* Adam, but man, as in the *human race* or *mankind*. In this covenant, God committed Himself to partnering with man in manifesting His will in the earth. Man's right of dominion in the earth is a result of a Covenant that God bound Himself to with man, which requires him to partner with him on matters relating to the earth.

Owner and Possessor

Man's right to dominion in the earth is not an inherent one, but is a right granted him by the same covenant that limits God's activity in the earth without his participation or agreement.

When conceptualizing the balance between God's ownership of the earth, and man's dominion over the same property, we can utilize the relationship between a landlord and tenant to help us understand this relationship between God and man.

To begin, the landlord and tenant relationship is a legal one, which is created by a legal agreement. The landlord does not relinquish ownership of the property, only its possession, use and enjoyment of it for the term established in the agreement, lease or covenant with the tenant. The tenant has no ownership interest, but stands in the stead of the owner in his possession and protection of the property against third parties that would damage or destroy it. During this proscribed period of time granted the tenant, the landlord is limited in what he can do with his own property without the tenant's permission. Once the terms of the lease are up, the owner retakes possession of his property unhindered.

Implied Covenants

In reviewing God's activity in Genesis 1, prior to the creation of man in verse 27, I recognized some very strong similarities in the approach God took in preparing the earth for man's arrival and the preparations a landlord is legally required to take for the arrival of a tenant. To begin, the legal relationship between a landlord and tenant is include covenants that are implicit, which means that they do not need to be written in the agreement in order for them to apply to the parties., because they are implied by law. One such covenant is known as the *"Implied Covenant of* Habitability. This implied covenant requires that the landlord make the property suitable for the purpose it is being rent or leased for. This means, if a property is to be used as a residence, then the landlord is responsible to make it habitable or suitable for that purpose. In looking at Genesis chapter 1, this is exactly what God did for man, before moving him into his place of dominion (see Genesis 2:7, 15). The Bible describes the condition of the earth in Genesis 1:2 as being:

> *"Without form, and void; and darkness was upon the face of the deep. And the Spirit of God moved upon the face of the waters."*

The earth in this condition was uninhabitable. However, God's purpose for approaching the earth at this time was to establish man in the earth as its ruler for the purpose of advancing and manifesting His heavenly Kingdom on earth. Therefore, God over the next 6 days is engaged in renovating and restoring the earth to a condition in which man could live. Once the earth was in a condition that human beings could habituate it, only then did God enter into covenant with man and give him his place of dominion.

Implied Covenant of Quiet Enjoyment

The covenant of *Quiet Enjoyment"* is also an implied covenant, which means that it is implicit in every residential agreement, and likewise does not need to be written into the agreement itself. It basically ensures that the landlord / owner will not do anything with the property that will interfere with the tenant's ability and right to use and enjoy the property. The covenant specifically prohibits the owner of property from reentering or interfering with the tenants exclusive right of possession and enjoyment of the property. This means that the landlord, although the owner of the property, cannot use his keys and enter the premise without first being given authorization or permission to do so. Why is this? The answer is: The landlord has a covenant with the tenant that promises that he will not do anything to interfere with the tenant's use and enjoyment of the property. It is the landlord's own words or covenant that prevents him from taking these steps, not the tenant. The tenant's rights flow from the same covenant that legally proscribes the landlord's actions towards his own property.

In a like manner, God having covenanted with man, granting him dominion over His property, is restricted in His ability to reenter His property without authorization from the tenant. The Landlord owns the property but cannot dictate what goes on inside of the tenant's home, and must be given permission to reenter the property while the tenant is under lease. God owns the earth, but He gave man dominion over what takes place in it. Therefore, from a prayer perspective, God is limited in what He can do for us, without Him finding someone who will authorize His intervention or allow Him to do what is needed through them.

The Marriage Covenant

Finally, I want to close this chapter by providing another example of this principle that I believe most of us can relate to. I hope this example will establish a level of understanding of the laws that define and limit

God's ability to intervene in the affairs of His children when they are bound by a legal covenant that governs a certain area of their lives. This example is the *Marriage Covenant.*

As long as an individual is unmarried they are, from a biblical standpoint, under the spiritual covering of their parents - specifically that of their father. However, once their son or daughter enters into a marriage covenant with another person, the new covenant now controls the affairs that take place within that relationship. The parents never cease from being their child's parents. However, the parents' ability to intervene in the child's affairs is now proscribed by a covenant that governs their son or daughter's life, i.e. the marriage covenant.

The marriage covenant creates a new authority structure within the son or daughter's life. The parents no longer have the right or authority to simply enter into their child's life and fix their problems, without being granted permission or authorization. Even if the parents see something wrong or unhealthy in the marriage relationship, they cannot simply begin to rearrange things for the couple without being authorized to do so.

In a like manner, God through His covenant with His children is limited in what He can do in our lives without our authorization or permission. It's not that He doesn't care about our situation. Quite the contrary! He cares more than we can imagine. The truth is, God is a God of His Word and will not break it for anyone – including Himself. God's own Word has proscribed what He can and cannot do in the earth. He had a purpose in establishing this order, and man as the sovereign ruler over the earth, that furthers a larger plan of God.

We will see later in this book, that this revelation of God's commitment to His Word is necessary for us to have confidence in our prayers being answered. This revelation will equip us to pray more confidently and effectively, thereby manifesting in our lives God's glory as a witness to the world.

Chapter Four

Learning to Pray

*"And it came to pass, that, as he was
praying in a certain place, when he ceased,
one of his disciples said unto him, Lord,
teach us to pray, as John also taught his
disciples"* (Luke 11:1).

Contrary to popular belief, prayer is not something
that every believer is born (or reborn) knowing
how to do effectively. Initially, we inherit the tradition
of loved ones or those who introduced us to Christ.
However, in order to learn what is Biblical prayer we
must be taught how to pray, just as Jesus' disciples
were. It is interesting to note that the disciples asked
Jesus to teach them to pray *"as John also taught his
disciples to pray"*, and not as the ruling religious
leaders prayed. The thing that distinguished John and

Jesus' prayers from the religious community's was their *assignment*. Both, John and Jesus' assignment was to declare the arrival of God's Kingdom in the earth. Both came declaring, *"Repent for the Kingdom of Heaven is at hand"* – or *is here* (Mat. 3:2, 4:17). They were on official business to declare that the Kingdom of God has again been made available to men, instead of the maintenance of a religious tradition. This is why it was necessary to re-teach their disciples the proper focus and purpose of prayer.

Jesus' Kind of Prayer

Jesus' disciples saw Him pray often and the impact it had in His life. These men witnessed Jesus praying for hours before the day began, then witness Him perform various miracles in impossible situation with confidence, as if He knew what He was doing had already been accomplished. Convinced that Jesus' kind of prayer was distinctively different and powerful, they wanted to learn how to do what Jesus did. Therefore, they asked to be taught how to pray.

In reading the Gospels, it becomes painfully clear that the disciples needed instruction on how to pray. To begin, nowhere in the Gospels (Matthew, Mark, Luke and John) do we find a single instance of the disciples praying, prior to Jesus' crucifixion. I believe this is due to their reliance upon Jesus, not only for their direction, but to do all of their praying as well. In John 16, the Bible records Jesus speaking to the disciples when He said:

> *"And in that day you will ask Me nothing. Most assuredly, I say to you, whatever you ask the Father in My name He <u>will give</u> you. <u>Until now</u> you have asked nothing in My name. Ask, and you will receive, that your joy may be full. "These things I have spoken to you in figurative language; but the time is coming when I will no longer speak to you in figurative language, but I will tell you plainly about the Father. In that day you will ask in My name, and <u>I do</u> <u>not say</u> <u>to you that I shall pray the Father for you</u>."* (John 16:23-26)(Underline added).

Jesus basically tells his disciples that the time is coming when He will no longer do the praying for them, but they will have to pray to God themselves. In Mark chapter 9, Jesus had to cast a demon out, after His

⚖️ 57

disciples failed to do so, then later reveals why they failed at their attempt, when He explained:

> *"This kind can come forth by nothing, but prayer and fasting" (Mark 9:29).*

Jesus said that part of their problem concerned their prayer life.

If the disciples struggled in their prayer life and needed instruction on how to pray effectively, I'm certain there are many believers today needing instruction concerning praying the way Jesus prayed.

One reason I believe so many people struggle in their prayer life is they've made the same mistake the disciples did by relegating their responsibility to pray onto other's, such as pastors, intercessors or the church's prayer ministry, while they themselves have never truly learn how to pray.

Silent Prayer

Every prayer found in the Bible was recorded by someone who heard what the person praying said. Therefore, it could not have been a silent prayer;

otherwise, the person would not know what to write. If prayer were supposed to be a silent matter, I believe when the disciples asked Jesus how to pray, He would have instructed them to pray with their hearts or minds, or in a similar manner. However, He did not do this. Jesus instructed them to pray "after this manner", and then He proceeded *to say to them* the pattern for prayers. I understand that God can read our hearts and minds, but we were created to have dominion and to operate in His likeness.

In Genesis chapter 1, God exercised authority over the earth by speaking to it. One of the most powerful things a son of God can do is speak! We were created in the image and likeness of God, and endowed with the ability to speak like He does. Man being a spirit with a body, we act and exercise authority by speaking words; especially when what we say is what God has already said. Whenever Jesus cast a spirit out, He spoke to it. When He found Himself in the middle of a storm, He spoke to the wind and the sea and they obeyed Him. When He multiplied the fish and loaves, He spoke to them by declaring a blessing over it. Jesus told the disciples, *"whoever <u>says</u> to this mountain ..."* (Mark 11:23, NKJV, underline added). In this same verse, He declares that whoever speaks, and believes in his heart what he said, *"he will have whatever he says"*. Our words can be the difference between life and death, for the power of life and death are in the tongue (Prov.18:21).

Prayer and Protocol

In any government, there is a protocol for it citizens to follow in their coming before it to present a matter. This is particularly true when the government is a Kingdom. Protocol and process protect the time and resources of the government, while safeguarding the dignity of the government itself. When speaking of a king, protocol plays a more prominent role in how we approach him to present a petition. Specifically, since the king's word is law within his kingdom, and it is what the citizen places their trust in. A petitioner must find their cause in the king's word for them to have confidence in the king acting on their behalf. More specifically, the individual's cause should have at some level the advancement of the health, interest and welfare of the kingdom itself, for it to be a priority to the king. This is why we are told to *"Seek first the Kingdom of God and His righteousness, all those thing will be added to us" (Matthew 6:33).* This commandment tells us what God's priority is, and what we are to focus on in order to have our personal needs met. This reveals an substantive component of protocol in our prayers that is often overlooked.

Protocol in Prayer

Many of the prayers we pray actually violate protocol established in the Bible on how we are to approach God, because they are not Kingdom focused or they in a real sense accuse God of not having provided for us in one way or another. These are not intentional violations but are a result of not knowing that these protocols exist because of how we have traditionally been taught to pray. We will see, that coming before God with a list of needs and personal requests, complaints or without reverence is a major reason many of our prayers go unanswered. It is true that God is our Father and that we have been granted free access to Him, but God is still committed to honoring His word concerning what He can and cannot do without our participation. Therefore, if our list of personal needs, concerns or complaints can be resolved by our exercising discipline or by seeking our answers, instructions and wisdom in the Word He has already revealed, God is not obligated to do anything further. He has "provided" the answer and we are responsible for using what He has provided to manifest the provision in our lives.

There are several points of protocol that we find in scripture that can lead us in how to properly pray as a citizen of God's Kingdom.

Protocol 1: *Base your prayer on God's Word*

It must be remembered, that God does not answer our prayers because we are in need, but to uphold His Word. God has already provided for all of our needs before they came to our attention. Our need is not for provision, but the wisdom on how to come into possession of that which God has already provided. However, when we find ourselves in apparent need because we have obeyed God's word or sought His Kingdom first, He will move for His Name and Words sake. He will not allow His Word to fail. Therefore, if my need is a result of obedience or the advancement of God's Kingdom, my concern is God's personal concern, and He will move heaven and earth to ensure that His word does not fail or return to Him void, having not performed what it was sent for. In summary, we must base our petition or prayer on:

1. What God has already said and promised, and
2. The advancement of His Kingdom.

Jesus promised, if we seek first God's Kingdom and His righteousness, that is His faithfulness to His Covenant Word, all things we have need of will be added to us (Matthew 6:33).

Protocol 2: *Never come before a king with complaints.*

Psalms 100:4, gives us a description of how king David

said we should enter the presence of "The King".
Specifically it reads:

> *"Enter into His gates with thanksgiving, And into His courts with praise. Be thankful to Him, and bless His name."*

This is the protocol for coming before a king. We see this truth demonstrated in scripture, in the Book of Nehemiah. Nehemiah heard of the dilapidated condition of Jerusalem and became very sad. He was a cupbearer to King Artaxerxes and knew that it was dangerous for him to appear before the king with a sad countenance. Therefore, the Bible says that Nehemiah became dreadfully afraid (Nehemiah 2:2, NKJV). Nehemiah understood the protocol concerning appearing before a king with complaints or in a manner that does not reinforce his dignity. Therefore, David admonishes us to come into God's courts with praise.

Religiously, we have been taught to come into God's presence with our problems and not with praise. We issue our needs and complaints before the Lord without showing the proper reverence. This is in most part due to the lost revelation that He is a King, as well as our Father.

Protocol 3: *We must always respect the King's Position*

This element of protocol is demonstrated in Jesus' Model Prayer were He immediately acknowledges God's position as "Our Father", as well as, His position as being a King with a kingdom. Our position as children of God does not absolve us of honoring Him as King. The Bible gives us an example of how the balance between God being a King, as well as, our Father can be maintained in the story of Queen Esther. Queen Esther respected and honored her husbands as king, although she was married to him. Queen Esther became aware of a plot to exterminate the Jewish people and her uncle advised her to make the king aware of this plot. However, to do so would require her to violate protocol and appear before his presence without being summoned. She recognized, by her violation of protocol, that the king did not have to hear her request, and it could also cost her life.

The text reads:

> *"And thus I will go in to the king, which is not according to the law; and if I perish, I perish. ... Now it came about on the third day that Esther put on her royal robes and stood in the inner court of the king's palace in front of the king's rooms, and the king was sitting on his royal throne in the throne room, opposite the entrance to the palace. When the king saw Esther the queen standing in the court, she obtained favor in his sight; and the king extended to Esther the golden scepter which {was} in his hand. So Esther came near and touched the top of the scepter. Then the king said to her, "What is {troubling} you, Queen Esther? And what is your request?"* (Esther 4:16; 5:1-3).

The king extends grace toward Esther and heard her request. However, the point here is that Queen Esther recognized that being related to a king, does not invalidate the laws that he has established upon which his kingdom operates. Likewise, God is our Father, but He is also a King. He has established laws within His Kingdom, upon which it operates, that we are not exempt from just because we are family!

Chapter Five

The Lord's Prayer Pt. 1

*"For your Father knows the things you have
need of before you ask Him."*

This revelation should cause all of us to pause and take notice. How could this be? Why would God know we have needs and do nothing to fulfill them? The answer lies in, what I have pointed out earlier in this book: God does not respond to prayers based on need, because He has already provided for them. Our issue is how do I come into possession of what has been provided. In the book of James, he gives us the answer on how to possess what God has provided, when he wrote:

> *"faith worketh patience. But let patience have her perfect work, that ye may be perfect and entire, wanting nothing If any of you lack wisdom, let him ask of God, that giveth to all men liberally, and upbraideth not; and it shall be given him.*

The answer is *faith, patience and wisdom*. Faith, being our taking legal possession for that which the Word of God has revealed as belonging to us; *patience* being our ability to rest in the revelation of having received by faith what God has provided, and *"wisdom"*, *being the know how, in what to do* in order to manifest that which has not manifested yet.

Asking

The Apostle James wrote in the epistle bearing his name, *"You do not have because you do not ask"* (James 4:2b). If this is true, and it is God's will that our needs be met, then why are we required to ask for things in order for our needs to be met? The answer is found in the fact that by asking, we are at the same time granting permission for God's involvement. Remember, that God has given man dominion, which is absolute authority over the earth and what manifests in it. Therefore, using the analogy of the relationship between the landlord and tenant used earlier, if something within the apartment (the earth) is not working the way it was intended, the tenant (man) must notify the landlord (God), that something needs fixing, and that he (the landlord/God) has permission to enter the apartment (the earth) to do so. The issue is not that the landlord (God) did not provide what needs to be fixed, but that the agreement requires the tenant to notify the landlord if something he has provided needs fixing. God requires that we recognize Him as our source. He knows what we need and how to properly address apparent lack or insufficiency in our lives. He will either send a word or a person who possess the insight or wisdom needed to resolve the situation. In other words, asking sets in motion the forces and people that God has set in place to assist those in covenant with Him, in having their needs met. Make no mistake, anything you receive from a job or person, ultimately came from God. They were simply the means or resource, used by the Source, which is God, to get to you what He has provided. James declared that:

> *"Every good gift and every perfect gift is from above, and cometh down from the Father..."* *(James 1;17).*

Therefore, when we ask God in prayer for something, it is not because He has not provided it, we are really asking for what has been provided to come into our possession.

Asking Amiss

The apostle James points to another reason many of our prayer go unanswered, even when we ask when he said:

> *"Yet you do not have because you do not ask.*
> *You ask and do not receive, because you ask*
> *amiss, that you may spend it on your pleasures"*
> *(James 4:2-3, NKJV).*

James points out that we are asking, but they are not in line with God's priorities. They are selfish and serve to advance only the individual's interest. This is why we are not to pray for our needs, if they are not promised in God's Word or needed to advance His Kingdom. When we seek first the Kingdom of God and His righteousness, and we encounter a need, it truly is not our need, but God's. We are His hands and feet in the earth carrying out His will. Therefore, He is responsible for providing us with the means to accomplish our assignment. It is a law within the Kingdom, that: "Whatever God' requires of us, He must first provide us." Therefore, a prayer for the purpose of manifesting His Word or advancing His Kingdom is one that we can have confidence it will be answered. The purpose of our prayer, determines its priority in the Kingdom. If our asking is to advance God's purposes, then it is a high priority and is properly a demand upon God to act in our situation, in which He must respond. If it is a prayer where we are asking amiss or to fulfill a purpose, that if answered, would advance only our own interests, then we are actually begging and God is not obliged to answer it.

The Middlemen

I have discovered that many of our prayers go unanswered, not because God has not provided, nor because we have not sought Him reverently or for the right purposes, but because God has to use other human beings to obey Him in getting to us what He has already provided. In other words – disobedience! Our lack or needs may be a result of someone disobeying God in their stewardship of what He has provided for us.

Due to the law of dominion requiring God to use human beings in order to manifest His will in the earth, He has to use them to answer prayers that involve natural resources or opportunities in the earth. Oftentimes, these stewards of God's resources have their own interests that get in the way of them obeying God's leading in releasing that which they are in possession of, so that they can meet the need for which God originally provided them for. This includes both saved and unsaved individuals, institutions and organizations. As a result, prayer may be delayed in being answered because of someone or something resisting the will of God.

Our Model for Prayer

In Jesus' model prayer, he told His disciples:

"After this manner therefore pray..." He did not say, *"pray this prayer"* or *"memorize this prayer".*

Jesus did not instruct the disciples to pray whatever was on their hearts, but to pray *after this manner*, this *pattern* or this *fashion.* This is important because it insinuates that there is both a priority and manner that is appropriate to bring before God. Just because there are not specific instructions on what we are to say in prayer, it does not mean that there is not a standard of prayer that God deems acceptable, especially when it is a prayer requesting that He do something for us.

This truth is demonstrated in Genesis chapter 4 where God chastises Cain for making his offering to God in an *unacceptable or unauthorized* manner. Specifically it reads:

"And in the process of time it came to pass that Cain brought an offering of the fruit of the ground to the Lord. Abel also brought of the firstborn of his flock and of their fat. And the Lord respected Abel and his offering, but He

⚖️

*did not respect Cain and his offering. And Cain
was very angry, and his countenance fell. So
the Lord said to Cain, "Why are you angry?
And why has your countenance fallen? If you do
well, will you not be accepted?"* (Gen. 4:3-7,
NKJV).

Nowhere in scripture is it recorded where God gave
Cain and Abel specific instructions on how to bring
their offering or what to bring as an offering. However,
it is evident from God's response, that there was a
standard by which an offering would be considered
acceptable or unacceptable. Objectively, there
appeared to be no distinction between the two brothers.
They were both sons of Adam, living within a fallen
system and dependent upon God for their needs to be
met. Both brothers brought an offering, but one
brother's offering was received as acceptable, while the
other's was not. Therefore, there had to have been a
standard established by God on how they were to
approach Him.

Likewise, Jesus' *blueprint* for prayer reveals a
priority in our prayer, along with certain elements and
characteristics of a prayer that is acceptable to God.

Whether or not we pray according to God's revealed will, can determine our effectiveness in prayer.

Our Father's Name

> *"Our Father in heaven, Hallowed be Your name."*

It is interesting to note that Jesus chose to refer to God as a "Father". Biblically, the name of a person embodies the essence, destiny or purpose of the person. When Moses asked God for His name, God responded with the name, *"I AM THAT I AM"* (Exodus 3:14). In essence, God was saying to Moses: *"You cannot confine or define My being with a name because I am so much more than your mind can imagine, tongue can articulate or language communicate. I AM whatever is required or I choose to be. This is what I AM."*

In Jesus' pattern of prayer, He establishes that our first priority and focus in prayer should be *God* and *His Kingdom*. Therefore, when Jesus said that we are to address God as *"Father"*, He is indicating that we are to recognize Him as being our Source.

Before we ask anything of God we must reverence and recognize Him as our Source (Father) and Sovereign (King). By doing this we can place our confidence in faith where it belongs – in God!

The King and His Kingdom

"Your kingdom come."

Jesus identifies "our Father" as having a kingdom, which designates Him as a King. Jesus says that our prayer should be, that *"His Kingdom come and will be done on earth as it is in heaven"*. This is consistent with Jesus' command in Matthew 6:33 and Luke 12:31, that our primary pursuit in life is to *"seek first the kingdom of God."* As a result, everything we need will be added unto us.

As mentioned earlier in this book, the primary responsibilities of a citizen in a kingdom is to:

1. Maintain their "allegiance to the King.
2. Obey the laws of the kingdom, and
3. Support the advancement of the Kingdom.

Therefore, this prayer identifies us as citizens coming before our King.

Jesus came announcing that the Kingdom had come or is again available to men (Matthew 4:17). Therefore, every time we pray: *"Let your kingdom come, Your will be done on earth as it is in heaven,"* we enter into agreement with the will of God and give Him authorization to use us to manifest His will in the earth. Again, this prayer is a pattern, not a memory verse, to give us insight into how we come into agreement with the will of God, and partnering with Him in manifesting it in the earth.

Your Will

"Your will be done ..."

Knowing the king's will is the key to answered prayer. Therefore, when Jesus instructed the disciples to pray for God's kingdom to come, and for His will to be done, on earth as it is in heaven, He was taking their focus off of themselves and placing it upon God's purposes. God's will is expressed and revealed in His Word. This is why we must know the Word of God. The will of a king is found in his words. The words of a king are the laws of his kingdom. Therefore, when we know the king's words, we also know His will. Once we align ourselves with his will and commit ourselves to his words, we have a right to expect the king to protect his word from failing, thereby protecting us from failure as well.

The Apostle John wrote that this is how we come to confidently pray! Specifically, he wrote:

> *"And this is the confidence that we have in him, that, if we ask any thing according to his will, he heareth us: And if we know that he hear us, whatsoever we ask, we know that we have the petitions that we desired of him" (1Jo. 5:14-15).*

Again, the will of a king, is his revealed word, and the word of a king is the law of his kingdom. Therefore, when we base our prayers on the will of the king, he is personally committed to performing his word. The prophet alludes to this fact, when he wrote:

> *"So shall my word be that goeth forth out of my mouth: it shall not return unto me void,*

but it shall accomplish that which I please,
and it shall prosper in the thing whereunto I
sent it" (Isaiah 55:11, KJV).

To truly understand what God's will is, we must look at how things were in their original state, before man frustrated God's will through rebellion and sin. In this original state of being, there was no lack, insufficiency, disease, pain, suffering, death or oppression. All of these are contrary to God's will.

The Apostle John, being led by the Holy Spirit, wrote:

"Beloved, I pray that you may prosper in all
things and be in health, just as your soul
prospers" (3John 1:2).

This is why God sent Jesus to "restore" His will in the earth by making available to us the wholeness we lost in the garden, which can only be found in His Kingdom. Therefore, we pray: *"His kingdom come and will be done on earth as it is in heaven!"*

Heaven on Earth

"On earth as it is in heaven."

I believe there is a lost revelation of God's will, found within the Lord's Prayer, that we must rediscover. This revelation is: *God desires for the earth to be a reflection of heaven!* That's right – Heaven on Earth!

As we discussed in previous chapters, God created a kingdom for man to live in. This Kingdom was established in the middle of a garden that was named Eden. As referenced earlier, a name defines and describes the essence or substance of the thing named. The word "eden" translated means *pleasures* and *luxury*. Therefore, when God created His garden kingdom, it reflected the environment He intended man to live in – *pleasure and luxury!* This was the original intention of God for man manifested on earth. God did not create man and place him in a desert. He could have easily done so if that was His will for us; living day by day, paycheck by paycheck, continually struggling with lack and insufficiency. However, He did not do this. God purposefully choose the conditions, environment and government in which man would live in the earth, to reflect that which already existed in His heavenly Kingdom!

Access to Heaven

In the truest sense, prayer is a means established by God, by which heaven gains legal access into the earth, and earth gains access to heaven. Jesus, in Matthew 16:19, tells Peter that he has been granted authority to access heaven for the purpose of manifesting it here on earth. Specifically, Jesus said:

"I will give you the keys of the kingdom of heaven; and whatever you bind (declare to be improper and unlawful) on earth must be what is already bound in heaven; and whatever you loose (declare lawful) on earth must be what is already loosed in heaven" (AMP).

Keys represent both access and authorization to whatever the keys belong to, in this case heaven, i.e. *"keys of the kingdom of heaven"*. Think about it from this perspective: by giving someone keys to your car, you have both authorized them to drive and possess everything in the car. Jesus, in making the above declaration to Peter, and subsequently the other disciples as well (see Matthew 18:18, explained that they were authorized to permit on earth, that which was already legal or permitted in heave, and they were responsible for forbidding on earth, that which is already forbidden or unlawful in heaven. Jesus in a real sense has commission the believer to implement heaven's laws on earth. The reason for this is found in the fact that laws create culture. By taking the laws of heaven and implementing them here on earth, we are cultivating or manifesting heaven in the earth

I have heard others interpret this text to mean, *"Whatever we bind on earth, shall be bound in heaven, what ever we loose on earth shall be loosed in heaven"*. This is distorts the verse true meaning on several levels, and gives the impression that we legislate what takes place in heaven, when our dominion has been proscribed to the earth.

I believe the King James Bible translators translated the text this way in order to avoid the theological implications. However, the text is plainly written in the *"perfect passive participle"*, which indicates an action that has *already* taken place – past tense. Therefore, the believer is reflecting upon what has already taken place in heaven and establishing that in the earth. We must remember that heaven is the original and earth is the image. As it is with confession, we must agree with and say what God has already said. The prayer is for God's Kingdom to come and His will be done on earth as it already is in heaven.

Another reason this translation or understanding of this text is incorrect is that man has not been given authority to legislate in heaven, but the responsibility of manifesting it in the earth. God has already taken care of that establishing His law in heaven and does not need us to amend or add to it based on what is taking place here on earth. Our authority concerns matters that take place here on the earth and bring what has already been done and established in heaven to earth!

Chapter Six

The Lord's Prayer Pt. 2

Deliverance

"Give us this day our daily bread."

This section of the model prayer is primarily premised on our need for deliverance from the consequence of man's fall from God's Kingdom.

Now that God and His Kingdom have been recognized as our focus and priority in prayer, Jesus then turns our attention to how we are to approach manifesting the things we stand in need of. As mentioned earlier in this book, the actual "prayer" is one of the last components of a formal petition brought before a court.

Prior to the prayer our petition consists of a:

1. **Jurisdictional Statement**, which recognizes the court's authority to hear the matter.

2. **Statement of Standing**. The petitioner establishes their right to bring their causes before the court.

3. **Recitation of the Law**. This focuses the courts attention on the legal basis of the petition's claim, to which the petitioner claims to have the right to ask the court to act on their behalf.

4. **Application of Facts.** The petitioner demonstrates how their situation falls within the protections given by the law.

5. **Prayer:** The petitioner, having establishes all of the above, makes a formal demand for relief by the court acting on their behalf in order to uphold the law it established.

Parts 1 through 4 are all satisfied in Jesus original pattern of prayer. Specifically, we recognize God's jurisdiction over us by declaring Him "our Father".

This is an admission of His authority, as well as, responsibility for us as His children. As His children, we are also citizens of His Kingdom, and therefore have "standing" before Him to have our petitions heard. By requesting that His Kingdom come, and His will be done, which is His law and word, on earth where we live, we are both recognizing His law and that it applies to us as citizens of His Kingdom.

The remaining part is the prayer, which is the formal demand for relief or authorization for the court's / king's intervention in our situation to protect their word / law. Jesus said that as citizens, if we seek the Kingdom first, that all our needs will be added to us. Therefore, the "prayer" portion of Jesus' pattern prayer begins when He instructs us to place a demand on this right. This is a demand; because it is what our King has promised and we have aright to its manifestation in our lives. Therefore, Jesus says that we are to demand: *"Give us this day our daily bread"*.

Notice that Jesus says that it is to be "given" to us, and in verse 33 of this same chapter, He promises that our provision will be "added" to us. The implication is that we do not toil for or earn these things, but they are benefits of our citizenship. They are our rights!

God sees us as citizens of a Kingdom whose primary pursuit is its advancement in the earth. This portion of the model prayer is the first section that legally qualifies as a "prayer", while the other portions comprised the protocol.

Daily Bread

This revelation of God's provision was lost when man lost the Kingdom, and had to now earn his living as a result of his fall.

As a matter of fact, God reintroduced His chosen people to the reality of sweat-less provision when He delivered them from Egyptian bondage. Upon entering the wilderness, God began the process of instructing the people on what it means to be a citizen of His kingdom. As slaves, the people had to work for their daily bread. If they did not work, they did not eat. This was the case for mankind in general without a covenant with God. However, God wanted to teach them that their daily bread was not a consequence of how hard they worked, but a benefit or right they have as a result of their covenant with Him. Therefore, He brings them out into a wilderness where they cannot care for themselves to establish in their minds that He is their Source!

In Exodus chapter 16, we see God teaching His people this as they wandered through the wilderness. Specifically, the text reads:

> *"This is what the Lord has commanded: 'Each one is to gather as much as he needs. Take an omer for each person you have in your tent.'" The Israelites did as they were told; some gathered much, some little. And when they measured it by the omer, he who gathered much did not have too much, and he who gathered little did not have too little. Each one gathered as much as he needed. Then Moses said to them, "No one is to keep any of it until morning. However, some of them paid no attention to Moses; they kept part of it until morning, but it was full of maggots and began to smell. So Moses was angry with them. Each morning everyone gathered as much as he needed, and when the sun grew hot, it melted away"* (Exodus 16:16-21, NIV).

God had to break them of the slave mentality they developed while in captivity. God was introducing them to "Kingdom living", which does not involve toil and labor in order to have our needs met. This is why God specifically told them not to save any of the manna for the next day. He wanted them to develop trust in Him and their covenant, as well as faith in God's Word as being sufficient for them..

God likewise wants to deliver us from worrying about having our needs met. Jesus said that we have a right to demand these things as citizens of His Kingdom who have a covenant with God. We must first seek God's Kingdom, and ask that it be manifested on earth, as it is in heaven, where there are no needs. As a consequence, we have a right to have our daily needs met and can "pray" with confidence that *we have the petitions that we desired of him*" (1John 5:15).

Deliverance from Debts

> *"And forgive us our debts, as we forgive our debtors. And lead us not into temptation, but deliver us from evil."*

At this place in the Lord's instruction in prayer, we are commanded to forgive debts as ours have been forgiven, and that we would not be lead into temptation. At first glance, it appears that Jesus is speaking of the forgiveness of sin, lest we fall into temptation. However, this is not the case, because He specifically addresses sins after He finishes the model prayer, for at verses 14 and 15 He says:

> *" For if ye forgive men their trespasses, your heavenly Father will also forgive you: But if ye forgive not men their trespasses, neither will your Father forgive your trespasses."*

What is Jesus specifically referring to when He speaks of debt and temptation? To understand this, we must look at the following verses because they all concern addressing the consequence of man's loss of God's Kingdom. When Jesus speaks of forgiving debt, He is speaking of indebtedness, for we are to *"owe no man anything but to love him"* (Romans 13:8). Jesus is speaking of our having made promises to God and others and not followed through on them. These are debts, that God had to forgive us of, and we likewise are required to forgive others.

Temptation

This leads us into the next concern listed by Jesus, in reference to not being led into temptation and delivered from evil. To begin, the Bible plainly states God tempts no man with evil. The Apostle James wrote:

> *"Let no one say when he is tempted, "I am tempted by God"; for God cannot be tempted by evil, nor does He Himself tempt anyone"*
> *(James 1:13).*

Therefore, the translations that renders the text to mean that we are to ask God not to lead us into temptation has been misinterpreted in light of the context of the verse. It should be read to mean, don't allow us to enter into or be tempted. Temptation is an indication of lack in a given area of life. A person is not tempted in an area where the need is being met. Therefore, this deliverance is from having needs. This supports the verses spoken by Christ, both before and after this text. Being in debt opens one up to various forms of temptation, either by doing something unethical or that violates one's conscious, or the temptation not to honor the debt. Both cause the individual to become vulnerable to being temptated and ultimately sin.

A Revelation of Evil

"But deliver us from evil."

It is important to not only look at the order of the prayer Jesus taught, but also the terminology used in the prayer to gain an understanding of what He actually meant. It is interesting to note that there are approximately 10 different words used in the New Testament that are translated *"evil"* and Jesus chooses the one that points back to the Garden of *Eden!* Let me explain.

When we study the word Jesus used that is translated *evil*, we discover that He was continuing His focus on the restoration of God's Kingdom being restored in the earth. Some Bibles translate the word used by Jesus to mean *"the evil one"* or *"evil" in a moral sense.* These are incorrect. The word used by Jesus is in the *nominative case*, which usually denotes a title in the Greek. Therefore, Jesus statement can be translated as saying, "deliver us from *"the evil"*. It is a specific kind of evil that in one sense or another characterizes all evil. The Strong's Concordance reveals that the word used by Jesus cannot be construed to relate to evil character, or degeneracy or lacking virtue.

Specifically, the word used by Jesus in the Greek is the word "poneros". Poneros means: to be hurtful, or full of *labours,* annoyances, hardships, pressed and harassed by labours bringing *toil.* This is important, because immediately it is referencing painful work. This word poneros comes from the word *"ponos",* whose base is the word *"penes",* which means to be *"poor".* Its root word is the word *"peno"* which means: *to have to toil for your daily subsistence or daily bread.* If we were to take these definitions and place them in the context in which Jesus' spoke them, we would discover that Jesus was instructing us to pray for deliverance from *"the pain of poverty and*

having to toil or work for our daily bread." Wow!
From a Kingdom perspective, working or toiling to
meet our needs is considered poverty! This is because
this was not God's original economy given to man.
Remember, Jesus had just instructed us to pray for the
kingdom to be restored and for our daily bread to be
provided

The presence of the words toil and bread, are both
indications that Jesus is pointing us back to Genesis
chapter 3 where man fell and lost God's Kingdom and
his benefits – covenantal provision!

In Genesis 3:17-19, the Bible says:

> *"Then to Adam He said, "Because you have
> heeded the voice of your wife, and have eaten
> from the tree of which I commanded you,
> saying, 'You shall not eat of it': "Cursed is the
> ground for your sake; In toil you shall eat of it
> All the days of your life. Both thorns and
> thistles it shall bring forth for you, and you
> shall eat the herb of the field. In the sweat of
> your face you shall eat bread till you return to
> the ground."*

In this text we see the very things Jesus said we
should pray to be delivered from: toil, pain

(represented by thorns and thistles), sweat and bread. It must be noted, that God originally gave man fruit and seed as his provision (See Genesis 1:29). Both reproduce without man having to earn or make it, especially with the blessing of God in full effect over the earth and man's work (Genesis 1:28). If man desired to eat a piece of fruit, it was not a loss, but actually released the ability to reproduce what was eaten several times over, due to the seed in what was eaten. However, now that ground has been cursed and told to withhold from man what he needed, until he invested sweat, toil and labor, we are introduced to something the Bible describes as "bread". Bread is not a naturally occurring resource in the earth It must be made through toil, and does not reproduce itself. It provides strength only for the day! Therefore, with the fall of man, his economy shifted from being based on seed to bread. Jesus instructs us to pray for restoration of the original economy, where our daily needs are given us, not earned as a result of our toil!

I am not advocating that believers walk into their job tomorrow and quit. No! That's not what

I am saying. What I am saying is that we should not be looking to them as being our source. God is our Source and we trust in our covenant with Him to meet our needs as we seek first His Kingdom! Our jobs are only a RESOURCE. God is our SOURCE! Therefore, we have nothing to worry about if we get laid off or the economy takes a turn for the worse. Our faith is in God!

The Kingdom

"For Yours is the kingdom and the power and the glory forever. Amen."

Jesus ends His model prayer the same way He began it by focusing on the King and His Kingdom. If I were to summarize the prayer itself, I would summarize it as follows:

1. The acknowledgement and reverencing of God and His Kingdom.
2. The desire for God's Kingdom and original intent for man be manifested in the earth, and
3. God the King owns all there is, including all glory, Amen!

Therefore, prayer is much more than a religious activity used to talk to God. It is: (1) an exercise of authority, (2) grant of authorization in and access to the earth (3) the petitioning of the King to act on our behalf. Understanding the laws and principles that govern God's ability to answer our prayers will cause us to be more effective at this very important right and responsibility we have as believers.

Prayer is official government business. We are the means by which the Kingdom of God is advanced in the earth. God needs "someone" with a *body* to give Him access to the earth to impact it with His will. This is why Jesus' model prayer is primarily a "petition" for God to have His way in the earth. Because the saying is true: *"Without God man cannot. Without man God will not!"*

Prayer of Salvation

If you would like to receive Jesus as your Lord and Savior, please repeat the prayer listed below.

"God my Father, I recognize that I have sinned. I confess and repent of my sin and desire to live for you. I receive Your Son Jesus Christ as my Lord and Savior. I believe that He died for my sin and that You raised Him from the dead to your glory. I receive by faith the finished work of Jesus on the cross. I receive and invite Your Holy Spirit to live in me. I thank you for your grace and Your Son! It is in the mighty name of Jesus I pray this prayer. Amen!

If you prayed that prayer please let us know so by contacting us at: jcmatthews.org or jcmatthews.international

Kingdom Conscious Prayer of Provision

"God, I thank you for having already provided for all of my needs according to your riches in glory. Therefore, I command those individuals, institution or organizations that you have placed in stewardship of the finances, resource, people, property, provision, opportunities and favor that I stand in need of, I command them to obey the voice of the LORD and release it NOW; so that the provision you have provided will come into my possession and meet the needs for which it was originally given. I thank you for it, and receive it by faith now - in Jesus Name – AMEN!"

Notes

_____

_____

_____

_____

_____

_____

_____

_____

_____

_____

_____

_____

_____

_____

_____

_____

_____

_____

_____

_____

_____

Notes

_____

_____

_____

_____

_____

_____

_____

_____

_____

_____

_____

_____

_____

_____

_____

_____

_____

_____

_____

_____

_____

Notes

About the Author:

Dr. J.C. Matthews is the
Senior Pastor of Reign
International Church,
formerly Dunamis Life
Ministries, and founder of
J.C. Matthews
Ministries, REIGN
Worldwide Inc,
The International Kingdom Institute (IKI), and the
International Association of Ambassadors (IAA).

J.C. has authored over a dozen books, the majority of
which are dedicated to understanding the concepts,
laws and principles upon which the Kingdom
operates.

J.C. has worked for some of America's top companies
prior to entering full time ministry. J.C. possesses a
B.A in Political Science, as well as a Juris Doctorate
(J.D.) degree. J.C. was twice a recipient of the
prestigious "Who's Who Among American Law
Students" Award (1996 and 1997) in recognition of his
outstanding study of law, in addition to
being honored as an Urban All-American by the
General Assembly of the Ohio State Senate.

Dr. Matthews brings a relevant revelation of the
Kingdom to the Body of Christ. His extensive legal
training and understanding of law and the Bible,
enables him to effectively communicate seemingly
complex concepts, laws and principles of the Kingdom
in a practical and simplistic manner.

Visit www.jcmatthews.international or www.jcmatthews.org

for more information and titles

  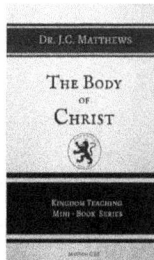